Myronn Hardy

The Headless Saints

New Issues Poetry & Prose

A Green Rose Book

New Issues Poetry & Prose
The College of Arts and Sciences
Western Michigan University
Kalamazoo, Michigan 49008

An Inland Seas Poetry Book

 Inland Seas poetry books are supported by a grant from
The Michigan Council for Arts and Cultural Affairs.

First Edition, 2008.

ISBN-10   1-930974-76-0 (paperbound)
ISBN-13   978-1-930974-76-0 (paperbound)

Library of Congress Cataloging-in-Publication Data:
Hardy, Myronn
The Headless Saints/Myronn Hardy
Library of Congress Control Number: 2007939664

Editor	William Olsen
Managing Editor	Marianne Swierenga
Copy Editor	Natalie Giarratano
Designer	Ephraim McNair
Art Director	Tricia Hennessy
Production Manager	Paul Sizer
	The Design Center, Frostic School of Art
	College of Fine Arts
	Western Michigan University
Printing	Cushing-Malloy, Inc.

The Headless Saints

Myronn Hardy

New Issues

WESTERN MICHIGAN UNIVERSITY

Also by Myronn Hardy

Approaching the Center

For Mom   Dad   and Erika

once again

Contents

V.

VI.

Il viaggio finisce qui:
nelle cure meschine che dividono
l'anima che non sa più dare un grido.

—Eugenio Montale, "Casa sul mare"

What one sees in this city at every step, turn, perspective,
and dead end worsens one's complexes and insecurities.

—Joseph Brodsky, *Watermark*

I.

Dive

Boats are whispers bobbing in water
so shallow each pebble acute.
What does night bring other than the moon?
Endless pacing   lonely or coupled.
The day leaving crowded heads.
Airborne salt filling lungs.

Jump into the sea   swim until it
gets deep. Dive for chests of silver   the lost
luck of pirates   bankrupt empires.
What you find may feed this town forever.

Lobsters: Arkansas, July 1983

I believe it was an anaconda   caged
propped on a wood stand. Asphalt hot

transparent waves undulating still air.
THE WORLD'S LARGEST SNAKE   the

sign chained to the rusted bars. There were
ticks on a black/brown/white figure eight

atop the head. Memory sucked into new
bodies. No thieves in the Amazon   no

burlap sack   mouth held closed with four hands.
I was small enough to push through the over

two-hundred crowd   lobsters in overalls   straw hats.
It looked dead perhaps playing such so all might

leave. It was thicker than me   length coiled
about the mesh floor. There were crocodiles

in its eyes   past battles   meals. A woman (lobster)
yelled *I need some pretty boots*. Did she

watch Turner's death? Ask for brown lampshades?
Were they all there   tongues long wet as worms?

When it really dies   will each try for a tooth? Place
in a box   pass it through a family.

This is who we are.

Premonition of June

First   I see blue then North
America. Bristles of old brushes
fall away leaving bones on this canvas.
As I make your birthday painting I listen
to your grandfather on the radio
attempting to find you   to inform
me of the eyes spread over the
Atlantic. Are they strangers'
from here or elsewhere?
Yes. We will visit Santiago.
Here it is a gray dot

on a long island. A place where I've
found everything. Perhaps it will be
the same for you   the bataá   congas
underneath Pegasus. Oh   the
women   the sea in their skin   palms
where lilacs bloom. This June will
be a door with an opal knob   turn
it then tumble into its house. Silver dust
will fall from a dragonfly's
wings as the sea ripples   wave
upon wave   dark opening light.

Hallelujah

Split crosses   skulls   daggers
tattooed on his arms   chest   most
are almost removed. *This is who I*
used to be. I shake his father's hand   little
finger gone in a welding accident.

His father came to Salvador from
Winnipeg   loved a woman until she had his son.
In the favela   he built her the largest house on the
highest hill. They stared at the puce road below where
Franciscan dogs   children played with rocks   sticks.

I sit in the living room with his father. He takes the
soiled fedora from his head   places it on his
grandson's. *This one will be a welder like me.* I smash
a mosquito on my neck   malaria will be back   I
will sweat for days.

On a tarnished tray   his daughter-in-law brings cups
of ice cream   places them before us. As we eat   I notice
wax masks on the cracked walls   each face vulgar in its elation.
Tomás   standing there right now all clean. You remind me of your
mother. Everyday she was an apparition in white clothes.

His grandson takes the hat off   places it on
his grandfather's head. *I had a hat just like this*
one   he stood up. *Let me go look for it.* His son kicks
the floor   the dirt hard as shells. *My father has*
had a difficult life.

Diffused mauve light from a broken
street lamp   we walk to the church.
His mother is on a distant beach tying Lent
rafts adorned with laelias   white candles.
They will float days after afoxé ceases.

Red ants crawl on the pews. We kneel
on velvet   colonial   threadbare. A
vase of plastic carnations   a
bronze cross are the only
embellishments on the altar.

The preacher tells us all to stand. I share a
bible with Tomás as he prays for a mother he
no longer knows. *Oh this country   this*
silver-clad battle within us   how will
we know its end?

Lorca, 1930

Siempre he dicho que yo iría a Santiago
en un coche de agua negra.
        —from "Son de negros en Cuba"

Each morning was a chocolate
croissant in the plaza. I'm watching

water fall over stone pomegranates
as nuns pass   crystal rosaries in waterless

fingers. I'm searching for a poem   perhaps
one with piety as the cathedral bells

crack the marble city.
This was your favorite place   mine

too   the maroon sun   the scent of almonds.

The African Film Festival at Lincoln Center:
Two Languages

—for Abderrahmane Sissako   Mahamat Saleh Haroun

1. In Hassānīya

The radio buried in sand is language.

Abdallah watches days in Nouadhibou
from a window the size of his forearm.
Sandaled feet where cloth hovers above
like time before a ship's departure.
He reads novels. Plots change with
perishable light. Silence makes all who
know him worry especially his mother.

Waiting in the living room his shirt matches
the curtains   sofa. The oddity of a face
disconnected   a mind in a continent
untranslated. He watches a girl practice
an old song with her mother. There
are ice shards in the arid air but
he is the only one who feels them.
Imbued in gloom   he waits for
day's black rose.

The orphan can help him unravel his
tangled tongue but it is better   easier
at least for Abdallah to remain
adrift   to ponder the native sand's formation.
In a tone of caution   he speaks to a woman
who'd left the city then returned.
Somewhere in Spain she tried to find
her daughter's father   *Our child is dead.*
She told him in a hotel after sex   a glass
of water   mutual desertion. How peculiar
is karaoke in Mauritania with a Chinese
man loving a microphone?
Was their baby conjured in that bar's ether?
Did their daughter rest in her father's (the singer's) hair?

When the woman falls asleep   Abdallah rests beside her.
He glides his hand against her arm but she isn't roused.
She is numb to the stranger.
The coast is calling.

.2. In Chadian

Our uncle   the musician rode to our
Koranic school to deliver the picture
our father mailed to us. We unroll it   *Tangier*   he says.
We hold it to the wall.

A horizon without birds but there is a sea
where we will jump   shatter glass with fingers.
The man we saw in a film was our father. Now he
sees water lapping a continent   no river
muck tasting Cameroon.
Why can't he see us?
Our poor mother has gone mad   language
pours from pores   nefarious silence.
The other boys are jealous but it doesn't matter.
My brother is ill. My father doesn't know his sons.

The deaf-mute girl in yellow will escape
from this place with me. I broke the promise
I made to my teacher. Will death lead me
wandering directionless roads fatigued? Will I be
the keeper of existences lost? My brother is
gone as is my father. I will find my mother
with the girl in yellow. We will make her sing.

II.

The Hunter

The dogwood has bloomed
pink   white flowers. Beneath
its fragrant canopy the rhododendrons
are short   green as anger.
A crow walks along the rotted
deck   calls twice. She wants to perch
in that blood tree but drags her one
unhealable wing   torn by a spotted cat
protecting his newly clawed sun fish.
Does she remember the cage opened
on a long passed Sunday? The rabbits
the boys named   fed broccoli   dead
beneath her feet. How that morning
their gray fur skinned. Only two bodies
picked about   beak wet with life.
How the boys cried on Easter. They
asked their father to unpack the shotgun
his father carried in oak forests
as the hounds sniffed clover ground
for squirrels   raccoons   opossums.
He ran his hands through their thick
hair   *No. We don't live in Arkansas.*
These aren't those days.
He took them to the creek   showed
them crayfish burrowing in drowned
earth. They watched toads leap into
crabgrass   dissolve.

Tea in Perugia: November 11-12, 2001

Here we are: Jordan   Djibouti   Egypt   Israel
Ethiopia   Cuba   Gabon   North America.
We take a photograph together before
tea is poured. It's too sweet but we drink
it anyway. We discuss colonialism. There
have been too many holocausts   peoples
obscured   elapsed. Even now tongueless
nations are vapor leaving nothing but salt.

Why are we all in Italy?

Most are students but I'm here to read poems   to
visit a Cuban poet   his first time in Europe. We
share narratives in Italian. Pasta with green
onions   butter   who made this? The nuns will
be so proud   this convent kept so holy.

> The plane fell due to birds trapped
> in engines. How their hearts must have
> shredded   bones relinquished strength.
> Dominicans heading to funerals in Santo
> Domingo   new relatives from the new country
> will follow the newly dead. Candles added to those
> already burning in the playground   an altar for
> the missing two months earlier   no graves
>   soot passing without notice. That same month
> days   I bought porgies   parsley   lemons   picked
> up the dry cleaning as a group inside listened
> to the radio. A friend in Cuba thought of me
> when he heard of my city's   country's wound.

I sit beside him afraid of future's rumble.

Jesse Garon Presley's Advice

I saw a Japanese man wearing my
brother's picture pinned through
the red   blue ribbon of his hat.

It was where a rooster's feather should
have been. He was walking on 34th
Street   7th Avenue. Vacation I assume.

Business overwhelming. Yes   my brother
might be America. He is for so many who
are still waiting to see him in a restaurant   a bar

in Wichita slumped over a cold beer. Does
anybody know I guided him to Beale Street?
I told him to learn from the coloreds. Dance like

them   sing like them   it will make
you rich   more famous than God.
Wasn't I right?

And another thing   he bought the purple
1956 Cadillac convertible for me. Its color
had nothing to do with grapes   crushed or

otherwise. It was what I looked like born the 8th
of January 1935   Tupelo   Mississippi. It was me
my brother was driving with   talking to all those years.

Discovery

She braided blue thread in
her hair   swam to
a new island. She ate wild
berries   seeds   roasted
fish until her son was born. She
taught him how to carry stars in
eyelids   how to find North   how
to smell storms four days away.

When she passes   he will set the
island aflame. Yellow tongues
will leap into the sky   turn it red.

There will be ghosts waiting to
devour his frail body.

There will be nothing left in this world.

Listening to See

I will live without doors or
windows   only eggshell walls.
Someone will play a piccolo outside.
I will hold my ear against the wall and
think of winter   white trees   frozen
water where I long to glide.

A noose of gardenias grows from the
cracked ceiling. 1968   long
before I was born   another dead
uncle. The smoke house will be torn
down. My grandmother will look
away as the boy with the wild hair rests.

Will I become that boy?

I have let my hair grow into
copper smoke   a nightmare
in each swirl. The world for me is
frightening. White cats in barren oaks
stare with Plutonian eyes. We are all
mutilated. Scars are valleys we must scale.

Unlike for James   Vietnam
is a place I will discover
temples wrapped in rubber
trees   monks with shaven heads
humming. I will keep the vines
from coiling about me.

I imagine the rusted roof on that gray
house   the pungent hickory gone   no
swaying body. There on the almost
floor   I see a faceless woman dressed in
white. She is drawing long crooked roads with
her fingers. This time someone will live.

Fellini's Peacocks: The Fall

after Satyricon

In a granite court a black horse roams alone.
Will night persist   four days with desert
wind   a white cloak of sand? The two
poets have no answers but do find a slave girl
from Abyssinia. She hides from them. Her braids
are rivers to a country drying up   her body a destroyed
temple they loot together in a bath of blessed water.

Soon they are forced to take an
hermaphroditic god through the desert
even though sick   the canvas carriage
unable to shield a lava sun. The god
rolls in rancid sheets unable to breathe.
The poets are waterless   animal
bladders dry with salt.

They speak
to the peacocks
in Latin. The birds
answer lusting
skin   the pleasure
of plucking such
from their sallow faces.

Tails dragging in the
court exhume marble
veins. Those peacocks
weep as if human.

The albino god dies.
Lightlessness is a trick of war.
Time amorphous   a cloudy
fiction   eyes sewn blind.

On a Bench: My Life

How did I believe life would change?

My choices so limited I had to conjure
something that reflected light. It's cold
in Venezia but I sleep on a bench
the sea will soon swallow.

Here in a small jacket I'm observed by a poet
wayward in his search for a canal through this mind.

Ethiopia.

Yes.

I'm from Addis Ababa. Family slaughtered by
a murder of ghosts. Some were visible with guns
others inside skin   arms   fingers   proud
lives were all they knew. This place
of cathedrals   Catholic saints but bodies
are still nailed down   carried through crowds.

Return.

Yes.

To the desert lush as cantos.
The green place where we shared bread is
all I need: my sister spinning about the room   dinner
of roasted fish   yellow lentils as my father
tells of his favorite student   my uncle in church
speaking Ge'ez.

We have prayed so many years.
We are scrolls tightly wound yet I'm the only one left.

Return.

Yes.

In this head is all I have. My warm-poor
country these feet will never touch. I hope the water I
cup   let go   will spill over desolate land.

Calvino's Aesthetic

1. The City

Time is a spool of thread unraveling.
In the city we balance ourselves
on these fine fibers. So few equilibriums lost   we
are apt to singular lines. Supple cotton   wire
inside plastic   a controlled pulse.

2. Botany

To catalogue every tree is to examine each
hair on one's head. Oh   if you have
none there   the body will do just fine.
Each leaf   color   thickness   bud   blossom
labeled in Latin. Lucid variety (well maybe
not so lucid all the time. Some study is involved
but there is most definitely variety) tedious maybe
but I love it   the universe in every cell.

3. Agronomy

Sugarcane is a terrible crop. I believe torching
the fields makes things worse. What will people
grow when this doesn't? My birth island may
starve but we hope to save it.

4. Joseph Conrad

He was the subject of my thesis at Turin. The jungle
is just as civil as civilization. Maybe jungles are
more so. Of course   savages always come from
sophistication   too much access to things unnecessary.

5. Neorealism

I walk in a field of sunflowers where moths drink
oil   taste pollen. After I sleep   I notice those
moths have changed to golden nymphs. I'm naked
as are they   sweet tongues rolling over whey.

6. France

San Giovanni   Santiago de Las Vegas are broken roads.
Good but now I must settle. Who am I against this concrete?
There is mass in these surroundings. I've found it in each snowflake
against cobblestone   a young woman's lavender hat with a silver
pen shaped as an apple. To stare is to see nothing.
It's in quiet observation where all becomes visible.

Seven Dreams of Hands

1. Good Friday

An iron nail through the center   too many
red rivers gone mad. Who are the men who

do such things? Is it for the families they
are trying to feed? Blood porridge is inedible.

Spotted skin   quickly   an illness that can't
be cured. Fingers shocked   crushed

bone   tetanus   wood wishing to recoil.
My God what have they done?

2. The Congo: Leopold's Factory

Green plants can't grow in Belgium.
A king has made all recede. Little

girl with buried hands   under what sky
do they grow? At night you pick

them from branches   how easily
they reattach to wrists.

The carved doll   a gift from a great-aunt   you
hold her   nothing taken away   no

ax   no infection   no pain.
Come morning a truck will pass through

with a cargo of white language on
fire: burn   burn   burn.

3. Laws of Marrakech

Steal bread   evidence on the wall.
The town square rinsed   sunned leather   noticeable
bones remain.

How simple this approach   crime with crime
                                               biblical law.
Disable the senses   everything dies.

4. The Recital

The concert hall   a single pianist with
too many hands plays an impossible song.

This can't be a human being   thoughts
too complicated   coordination from a

flickering place. Planetarium eyes focused
on ivory   fingers long as swords   who is

her father? Sweat glides from temples.
The crowd cheers as the curtain closes.

No encore yet there is begging   notes
distant as nebulas.

5. Sarah's Farewell

It was the last time she held my hand.
There were sirens in the surf singing. We'd

left them behind along with everything else.
Sand ending   water called to clouds were gray

gargoyles. Notebooks destroyed   sculptures
smashed to dust. There was nothing of value left.

Cancer invaded   fluid   copper spheres endlessly
gave up. Youth nothing in a white hall   brown
faces welcomed.

6. Tornado

Cuticles cut   he pulls as much soil from the
grave as he can. His little girl spun in a wind
funnel   the house lifted then dropped   no family.

Who watches us? Who decides when all ends? Balls
of turquoise leave his face but what's the use? Coffins
close   bodies break   rise unfettered souls.

7. The Artist: What's Wrong?

Sand leaves with wind if you let it.
The cracks between fingers
are where walls fall   thin to nothing.
Each grain a second lived   earth's over and over.
The boy plants oregano   such loose ground. It
grows like dandelions   will make these days pass.
He makes tea   turns its color then walks through
a neighborhood of gawks. Cars stop. Girls scream.
Who is that boy?

Snow Spectacle

Piazza San Marco filled with birds   water.
My reflection is stagnant as is
Marcelo's. We are so foreign   such

poets where many have
churned language. Water with its
impeccable memory will

freeze. Snow will follow.
I wish I could see with you   your
first sight of snow. It will perhaps be

similar to the pigeons in your hands   on
your shoulders   those quivering
bodies plump with seed.

For me   snow is underneath my skin.
I know its complex chill. The way it
sleeps in pine branches. How holy

wings form when we rest   arms
extended crushing white crystals
until smooth.

Oh Michigan   everything
so white in December. Even the rabbits
shed the color in their coats.

Will your eyes turn green when
those flecks fall? Will you wait
outside   eat apples until they stop?

Will you wish your woman were there   those
jewels on her face? Will you think
of home   snow falling

on cabbage palms in La Habana   a
succinct moment so all can see
this confetti world?

The Chaos of Slaughter

—for Marcelo Morales

Monkfish have violent heads.
Their mouths are asylums where
no one is quiet. Mullet   crimson
off-white   innocent. When they
take out the eels I remember a sea

garden   tulips with gestating
spines   Eve crawling to land
with a mouth of almonds. Do the
fishermen know there are
two poets in their midst   foreign

as well? We watch as gulls
circle   call one another to feast
but there will be none for them.
Women will buy until each fish
is gone. Only scent will remain

perhaps scales   fins   twisted
innards   slaughter. The ice
spread in stalls   cold as this
November. Glaciers
melt   everything spoils   onto

the next trawl. Rubber boots keep
their feet warm but we are cold
like their fish. Venezia   oddly
sinking. Could this city become
a post-Atlantis   inhabitants

in constant scuba suits bearing
tomatoes   rabe   bread in plastic
containers? Perhaps evolution will
render fins. These noble
fish   mammals will sell antiquated

blown glass. Dissolved traditions
are folklore conveyed in cold water.
Jade funnels   eroding arches   light
so different.   What to do
but choke   slowly?

III.

Waiting before Water

A green sail   a raft
from where a boy
throws his net. The day

before only two black
bass caught   placed
in a basket yet all who

came to the coast
were hardily fed. Fish
are so biblical unlike

the city behind him with
its amber lights   woven
crude bodies floating

in colonial rooms once holy.
The oil refinery
will keep those lights

safe but not us.
For hours water
folds under

itself   no
lobsters
in the traps   no

crabs. This is all the boy
knows but his father is
hopeful. His wife serves

a lunch of beans   rice   sliced
cucumbers. She hums staring
at luminous waves   her

bronze son melting.
On the promenade all I do is
listen   wind sometimes

with rain   blue beads
in an ashen sea. I wonder
if they've broken that variable

floor   cracked
it so we'll soon be
steam   a race akin to clouds?

Salt

Leave me in a place where no one lives.
I will watch the dirt unravel from tires   scarlet
twine desperate when all is gone. The sun will turn
this back to bark but I will still wage forward   mountains
on either side. With white eyes   I see a body of water
in the shape of a scallop shell. I fall drinking until
my tongue dries.

Who is this cured man? Why is he atop
a salt grove   dirty in uniform? I have placed
him beneath canary cloth.

Is this bus in Somalia or Ethiopia?
Is this life over?

They find my watch in a market where calves'
heads are sold for three hundred francs but
no one will find me.

Garnets for *Dando*

after a photograph by Bauer Sá

Those pale spots on your

face are planets you

will never see.

Sleep has scratched your

back. Those stones have

no mercy but it is the gun

in your mouth that will

kill you. Turned upside

down it will happen quickly.

After a night of shining shoes

garnets will cut the air.

Damsel Returns to Ithaca

From the fire escape   a young
woman (after reading Homer) believes

she sees Polyphemus toss the dazed addicts from
the building stoop. He roars looking at

her   an eye strewn with veins ready to burst.
Her cat is under the bed. Fear is radiation in her skin.

Her neighbors are suddenly sober darting about the street.
The blast of radios ceases. Dominos are calm

as cards   checkerboards   dice.
The cat refuses to leave the dark underbed.

(She can't convince him). Odysseus is
not here   no sailors. *Why*   she thinks   *here*

in a young city (old for this country) an ancient
creature   a cannibal. She is late for her train upstate.

Hasn't been home (where she grew up) in years.
No expendable income. Money for rent   loaves.

The beast (at least that's what she sees)
demolishes her door. She screams   grabs

her bag taking to the fire escape.
Wonder who? Wonder what?

She leaps to the ground.
Her cat is gone.

She saw the tail twisting about that gruesome mouth.
In tears but she will make the train.

Harlem has never been so clean.

Jean-Joseph Rabéarivelo, 1937

je vous reviens avec un coeur désenchanté!
—from "Chants pour Abéone"

Born in a pillaged capital   poor.
Wealth another life when my mother
danced in vanilla air.
My uncle read to me   I enjoyed his

voice   stories but left school to wander in a
tribe of dead men losing fingers   arms
the closer we came to the moon. I had
no money   really didn't mind. My wife didn't

either. Her father took photographs   cried
when they developed before him.
The French killed so many of us   claimed
our island   bodies.

Who were we?
When my daughter died   there was nothing.
My blood was venomous. I wanted
it drained   the lungs purged   no breath.

Poems were birds that hatched in my hands.
They perched   nested in the baobao
outside my window. At night they were
lilac   iridescent   sang shrill songs.

I couldn't sleep. I ran on oil soaked sand to
another earth   no red island. My father
hemmed the sky with silk thread   that new
land   a continent of wheat mutilated by

locusts   my back covered with bites   colonial
death. Cruelty is acid forever burning
the wound. A small taste in June   no
Paris   no country
    this dead language will ascend.

IV.

Café Society, New York

One olive in a glass where two ice cubes melt.
Strange Fruit.
In 1938 Abel Meeropol gave a poem to Billie Holiday.
Strange Fruit.
She asked him what *pastoral* meant.
Strange Fruit.
He was a communist.
Strange Fruit.
As a girl she was a prostitute.
Strange Fruit.
He knew Ethel and Julius Rosenberg and adopted their two sons.
Strange Fruit.
She was a heroin addict.
       Strange Fruit.
His wife recorded his song first.
       Strange Fruit.
She beat up two white men after one   with his cigarette   burned a
       hole through her fur coat.
       Strange Fruit.
He changed his name to Lewis Allan.
       Strange Fruit.
Holiday and Meeropol met in New York City.
       Strange Fruit.
How did an immigrant write a song about the South?
       Strange Fruit.
She was twenty-four when she recorded his song.
       Strange Fruit.

Three Studies of Hibiscus

1. Fountain Hill, Arkansas

Near the railroad track
where a small girl
ran   hibiscus has grown
taller than expected. Years
without the train's iron
wheels   roots sliced   water
off course. In the girl's
hair a blossom   heady perfume
a life of circles.

A house glowing for no reason
other than a full moon above
a corn field.
Who lives here now?

2. Santiago, Cuba

White chickens thin as vertebrae
pluck petals. Bruised flowers
don't bleed   they shed scent.
A pungent defense but they keep eating.
Frailty meets another   pollen sticks to
feathers   a new crop.

The sun setting is the core.
Leaves are hands   a country reaching.

Flower crowns are wounds about saints'
heads   jagged as thorns.

3. Bahia, Brazil

Coils about the blue gate leading
to the elderly almond tree.
Shallow water   a tide that won't
return. Pull water with green hands. Pull
until all submits. Stretch until limber rubber
vines. Pink buoys graceful as paper boats.
This delicate air of sweet oil   light
opaque cells   windows   earth
magnified   Darwin's selection.

1937

If lightening strikes again   will
Rome fall? The Axum Obelisk might

in Piazza di Porta Capena.
A seventeen-hundred-year-

old symbol   a
city's   country's accolade. Mussolini's

yearning displayed   the
world listless.

Sixty years in an occupier's ether   prison
but this is tradition   the fairness of war.

Was this the phallus il duce
couldn't sever   too stunning?

Those hundreds of Abyssinian
men rounded up   instant

castrati but no voices   death. He wanted
all the dark women he claimed repugnant.

Oh   a piece of a continent that couldn't be
had the first time. The world

in hysteric mirth   apathy.
A place of renaissance   mines

of marble in volcanic soil.
My dear friends   is fascism perennial?

Franklin

I am Franklin.
Of course his life began

before mine   he is a cartoon
character but those are only two

differences. He met Charlie Brown
on a beach. I think Charlie lost his

beach ball   Franklin found it   asked
if it were his   a friendship began.

Now I hadn't seen the sea until I was
twelve but that's a small thing.

*What a crooked sand castle Charlie Brown
but it will do. We will play baseball soon.*

*How non-political our friendship   my
existence. Should it be otherwise?*

*Two kids the same age on a beach
completely normal   at least to me. We*

*will spend days talking about our
grandfathers. I've almost memorized*

*the Old Testament   excuse me if I do
go on. This center fielder will*

*forever wear a blue sweater   red
sneakers   that's just the style I got.*

V.

The Headless Saints

Agave water crests
beneath azure. Black moths

return to hills   islands waiting
to lose their vapor coronets   snow

pines. I will spool each cloud
into thread   cloth   clothes.

We will walk quietly through
town   bare soles. There is so much

to search for   paradise
in poverty's hot house.

Chop indigo   smear the juice
on cement walls   tree trunks.

Remember seas   the salt
that preserved those bodies

washing to shore. They are headless
but have learned to walk   climb

coconut palms   a green sweet harvest.
How holy they are naked   born

in a garden without unnecessary knowledge.
In a church they gather. We watch

with hands covered in the stickiest blue
(no fallen sky). A pope has not

made us saints   we neither want
nor need one to do so but here in

this town of stars   the smooth
feet of our dead against this

burned ground   there is
enough light here.

Holy Submersion: A Quiet Act

The photograph in my hands   a gray
face   eyes are jewels where light shatters.
She stands at the foot of a ruined
convent   one hundred featherless birds
in the attic   mice in the cellar eating each other.
I knew her when she was a girl   thick
socks sliding down narrow legs of amber.
I stand at the river bank. Honey is saliva
overflowing in a scorched mouth.
Water   a quartz leaf destroyed over
unyielding rocks. The pines have lost their needles.

I wrote her name on a ribbon. She tied it
to her wrist   walked until day burned black.
Where did she go? How will
I find her again? Does anyone
remember the girl in the citrine
dress   the gold hoops swinging on her earlobes?
Perch leap   all of those with hooks piercing
iridescent mouths fling themselves
to muddy rocks. I drop the photograph
in the violent water.
She has made me feeble.

The Living

White gold crowns on water   green
swirls into cobalt   light pierces.

Coral broken   a heart with exposed
valves   arteries   veins severed by currents.

Seaweed circles legs but will not pull
another body under. This time it drags

a living man to shore.

The First Ghetto

1516

A yellow beret among black
hats worn in a kingdom of water.

A woman has died of syphilis.
The doctor couldn't help

her   a moonless sky. He made the
curfew just before the gates were locked.

Canals   islands all connected by
bridges   water is all that is free.

2001

Outside the Jewish quarter two poets rest.
One tells the other how he hates half of his
country   *purposeless lives   days without
language spinning into gems.*

Does he not know he speaks of the other poet?
No   not from his island but of his descent. Here
in a cold he's never felt   he churns
the past only to spill its purple muck into water.

His familial migration from Cadiz to Havana was not
tumultuous. Heads filled with sun   nothing else
until everyone turned brown (but not too brown
and definitely not black).

Come on   sugar is the cotton above us.

Cataracts, 1907

Who changed this blue?
Those pallid smoke lines smeared
with clay   crushed hemlock reminds me of illness.
Will I become sick?
Sight speckled   no clarity.
I can no longer see the cathedral. I know
it is where those lines end but the terra cotta
roof is gone. The maple grove the Virgin
guarded   colored leaves with climate is gone too.

Has Venezia overflowed in my eyes?
Its auburn light too much for these
brittle corneas? Umber strokes with
sable brushes indistinguishable from
crimson as are my sons' faces
from Pissarro's sons'.

Perhaps it is this bridge   pale   mottled strokes
of auburn where I see myself giving up.
The water below cold   murky.
I have become someone else.

The Fever

1. Something In Bahia

It is a ball in my head that won't
go away or shrink. The right side
of my face   painful   take this
cheekbone away   give it to the dog
that keeps bothering me. I've been told
to sleep but there are only nightmares.
Maps are as confusing as
leaves   each one slightly ambiguous.

2. Vespucci: Malaria His Last Discovery

Who was this boy who knew Michelangelo?
Was Firenze a small town then perhaps the same
today? Off he went to Spain as did Columbus.
The rich boy who collected books became
a navigator   nights of glass stars   a small
almost-telescope. Mars   the moon brought
him to the Amazon River.

So many letters written to a friend in Europe
(where else would he have friends?). What
a find   *I'm not in Asia. This place is new.*
Maize   blue feather clothes   the beginning
of exoticism   crude nobility   these letters
published in many languages.

Yellow sleep killed him.
Sweat on a sheetless bed   skin
peeled away in a green place.

3. *Carta Mariana*

To be creative is to make up names.
Even my own a combination of things I

love   lakes   wood   mills. Who is that
explorer? His new
world   a new European
refuge. The North   South   both pieces
joined by one Florentine name.

The Making

1.

Clouds are gray from too many fires.
I'd say most from forests where
everything over one hundred years
curls over   no virtuous breezes here.
But there is an orange moon. I bet
if someone were to peel it they'd
find an apple   fruit baskets
combine   an idiom devoured.

2.

Black hands release wisps of smoke
after Jesus tosses silver coins. The world
forgiven once again.

Who is the little girl spinning light
     jasmine petals? I guess no one
knows but that sphere will rise tonight.

Water Study

Boats mean we exist.
Water is everything. May it break
on soil   sculpt perfect specks.
Turn this place jade as leaves. Break
over stones   smooth palms   no
rough work only paper. Colorless salt
knows color   cerulean rising in rays. Shells are
the truth. Listen carefully   close
to the ear   there are bones everywhere.

VI.

The Black Eagle

He was useful installing
electric light poles.
His language of flight
as illusive as was our
victorious war.

The emperor was kind
in the aftermath of his
destroyed plane but had
to turn away from such
a sweltering beast.

In 1935 there was
nothing he could
do for the Ethiopian
air force but claim
us   our country

backward.
It was for this
reason Harlemites
yelled   *Judas*
upon seeing him.
Touring a white country
denouncing a black one

disgraced   melanzana
leaf   vine tongue   everything
distorted. A dark man as
informant to pale men.
They are all assassins

in a clay room.
Lions gutted   their skins
adorned mosaic floors.
This amateur pilot   parachute
jumper   Italian citizen.

Swapped his Trinidadian
name for a Neapolitan one.

Alas   it was our expectation.
Relayed by a tranquil man passing
around a bowl of olives   tearing
bread into pieces. *Listen to yourself
before the rooster crows.*

Waterlessness: The Sign

Skin   flakes of dry ice.
I woke up for water. I opened my
bedroom door to find a dead
finch   a ribbon of ants rounding
her   tropical ritual   death growing
in the body   there will be nothing left.

Sun belly   there was no more air
to push   soundless. No brush near
the sea to play within   undergrowth
has lost a planter. How will the bounty
grow   spread about an island where
plastic murders so many?

Was that a sign of an insular life?
A place bound in a tight ball   gold or fool's
gold   hollow days.

Her last seed will grow   root
quickly   stems pruned   precise.
Oh that poor bird in that hot house.
What voice does she have now?

As for the End

There's an embryo in tonight's
moon but it will never speak.
It's a child   nascent now
who will die when given up.
Still born   gray baby never willing
to open one eye   the living too depraved
for delicacy   hand of mush.
Lilies thrown high   fragrant air
that makes everyone sick.
Why are we all crying?

I was told to build a boat
but rain is already here. I have no
lumber   no one's around to help me.
Should I gather seeds   steal my
neighbor's dog   cat   place black
tetras in a bag of water   air?
I'm screaming in this rain. Clear
tongues are vicious when all
you want is to be dry. Save this
young man   all of these
lives need space.

Meeting, 1936

> *Negroes met to consider going to Ethiopia . . .*
> *to spill their blood in behalf of our native land.*
> —Walter J. Davis, World War I veteran

On 138th Street   Lenox Avenue I signed up to go fight.
The speaker's voice was a thick rope pulling me in.
There was no way I could leave the crowd   walk in

New York City without giving up my twenty-five
cents   signing my life into life.
All gold calves must be melted   poured into cupped hands.

Upstate   men trained during summer   exercised in maple
air   military skill radiant.   Amharic   French   I will
be taught   study until I blend into Abyssinia   until

North America is wiped from skin. If splattered   this blood
will bear plum trees in red earth   grow tall
in lapis lazuli sky.

My people   it has been too long.

Esperança

These muddy roads even after heat
are copper mines unearthed. Don't
pay any attention to shoes sinking
I will save you   wash soles until
all is forgotten. Where the grass is
flat   the long path through brush
constantly growing   changing
leaves to orange flex. Life is
over   nothing can stop such
precision.

Watch the old man walk from the
swamp to the beach. Those stalks
of bougainvillea bleed from his back.
Violet blossoms are souls we must
keep from being born   entering
bodies bound for ruin.
Watch the old man with the tattered
clothes as the beach swallows him.
It will happen suddenly. In fact
everyone there will see.

Skin of every brown soft with sun waving
water   sand   air facing the faceless
man carrying flowers to whom
for whom? Everyday barefoot. Everyday
a glimpse   pink in an scarlet sky. He
walks by fish stands   snappers on platters
who used to swim in the salty bay   buckets
of amber bottles   cold gold poured into warm
stomachs   all will sleep well tonight.

This willed by a dead woman through color.
She held her husband's hand when it spilled
from flowers. There on cold ground he
wept then walked:

> Esperança for this town   my wife's
> return or my return to her.
> Esperança for this poor island.

Dead babies who try hard to cry.
Esperança for this useless beauty
affluent at its center.

Notes

"The African Film Festival at Lincoln Center: Two Languages":
The first film referenced is *Heremakono*. It was directed by
Abderrahmane Sissako, born in Mauritania and raised in Mali.
The second film, *Abona*, is set in Chad and directed by Mahamat
Saleh Haroun.

"Cataracts, 1907": In 1907, Claude Monet first noticed the onset
of his vision problem while vacationing in Venice.

"The Black Eagle": Hubert Julian, born in Trinidad and migrated
to the U.S. in 1921, also know as "Black Eagle," was an early
supporter of Marcus Garvey. He was recruited to Ethiopia as the
emperor's pilot in 1930 but was found unable to fly and land a plane
satisfactorily (even though he claimed to be the only black person in
America with a flying license). He became an Italian citizen in 1936
(the first year of the Italian-Ethiopian War).

Acknowledgements

Café Review: "The Hunter," "Snow Spectacle," "As for the End"

Callaloo: "Listening to See," "Premonition of June"

Karamu: "Lobsters: Arkansas, July 1983"

Many Mountains Moving: "The Headless Saints"

Natural Bridge: "Meeting, 1936"

nocturnes: "Seven Dreams of Hands," "Discovery"

Obsidian III: "Jessie Garon Presley's Advice," "The First Ghetto"

Paper Street: "The African Film Festival at Lincoln Center: Two Languages"

Phoebe: "Calvino's Aesthetic," "Hallelujah"

Poetry Motel: "Esperança"

Tampa Review: "The Living," "Lorca, 1930"

Third Coast: "Salt," "The Making"

Versal (Amsterdam): "The Fever," "Holy Submersion: A Quiet Act"

"On a Bench: My Life." *Poetic Voices Without Borders*. Ed. Robert L. Giron. Arlington: Virginia, 2005. 99. (Anthology)

I wish to thank the Fundación Valparaiso, the Fundacião Sacatar, and the Djerassi Artist Program where many of these poems took root.

Also, special thanks to Cave Canem, an exceptional joy.

photo by Gerald Cyrus

Myronn Hardy is the author of the book of poems, *Approaching the Center*, which won the 2002 PEN/Oakland Josephine Miles Award. He has received fellowships from the Annenberg Foundation, Cave Canem, Instituto Sacatar, and Fundación Valparaiso. His poems have appeared in *Ploughshares*, *Callaloo*, *Tampa Review*, *Many Mountains Moving*, and elsewhere. He lives in New York City where he's completing his first novel.

New Issues Poetry

Vito Aiuto, *Self-Portrait as Jerry Quarry*
James Armstrong, *Monument in a Summer Hat*
Claire Bateman, *Clumsy, Leap*
Sandra Beasley, *Theories of Falling*
Kevin Boyle, *A Home for Wayward Girls*
Jason Bredle, *Standing in Line for the Beast*
Michael Burkard, *Pennsylvania Collection Agency*
Christopher Bursk, *Ovid at Fifteen*
Anthony Butts, *Fifth Season, Little Low Heaven*
Kevin Cantwell, *Something Black in the Green Part of Your Eye*
Gladys Cardiff, *A Bare Unpainted Table*
Kevin Clark, *In the Evening of No Warning*
Cynie Cory, *American Girl*
Peter Covino, *Cut Off the Ears of Winter*
James D'Agostino, *Nude with Anything*
Jim Daniels, *Night with Drive-By Shooting Stars*
Joseph Featherstone, *Brace's Cove*
Lisa Fishman, *The Deep Heart's Core Is a Suitcase*
Noah Eli Gordon, *A Fiddle Pulled from the Throat of a Sparrow*
Robert Grunst, *The Smallest Bird in North America*
Paul Guest, *The Resurrection of the Body and the Ruin of the World*
Robert Haight, *Emergences and Spinner Falls*
Mark Halperin, *Time as Distance*
Myronn Hardy, *Approaching the Center; The Headless Saints*
Brian Henry, *Graft*
Edward Haworth Hoeppner, *Rain Through High Windows*
Cynthia Hogue, *Flux*
Joan Houlihan, *The Mending Worm*
Christine Hume, *Alaskaphrenia*
Josie Kearns, *New Numbers*
David Keplinger, *The Clearing; The Prayers of Others*
Maurice Kilwein Guevara, *Autobiography of So-and-So:
       Poems in Prose*
Ruth Ellen Kocher, *When the Moon Knows You're Wandering;
       One Girl Babylon*
Gerry LaFemina, *The Window Facing Winter*
Steve Langan, *Freezing*
Lance Larsen, *Erasable Walls*

David Dodd Lee, *Abrupt Rural; Downsides of Fish Culture*
M.L. Liebler, *The Moon a Box*
Alexander Long, *Vigil*
Deanne Lundin, *The Ginseng Hunter's Notebook*
Barbara Maloutas, *In a Combination of Practices*
Joy Manesiotis, *They Sing to Her Bones*
Sarah Mangold, *Household Mechanics*
Gail Martin, *The Hourglass Heart*
David Marlatt, *A Hog Slaughtering Woman*
Louise Mathias, *Lark Apprentice*
Gretchen Mattox, *Buddha Box, Goodnight Architecture*
Carrie McGath, *Small Murders*
Paula McLain, *Less of Her; Stumble, Gorgeous*
Lydia Melvin, *South of Here*
Sarah Messer, *Bandit Letters*
Wayne Miller, *Only the Senses Sleep*
Malena Mörling, *Ocean Avenue*
Julie Moulds, *The Woman with a Cubed Head*
Carsten René Nielsen, *The World Cut Out with Crooked Scissors*
Marsha de la O, *Black Hope*
C. Mikal Oness, *Water Becomes Bone*
Bradley Paul, *The Obvious*
Jennifer Perrine, *The Body Is No Machine*
Katie Peterson, *This One Tree*
Jon Pineda, *The Translator's Diary*
Elizabeth Powell, *The Republic of Self*
Margaret Rabb, *Granite Dives*
Rebecca Reynolds, *Daughter of the Hangnail; The Bovine Two-Step*
Martha Rhodes, *Perfect Disappearance*
Beth Roberts, *Brief Moral History in Blue*
John Rybicki, *Traveling at High Speeds* (expanded second edition)
Mary Ann Samyn, *Inside the Yellow Dress; Purr*
Ever Saskya, *The Porch is a Journey Different From the House*
Mark Scott, *Tactile Values*
Hugh Seidman, *Somebody Stand Up and Sing*
Heather Sellers, *The Boys I Borrow*
Martha Serpas, *Côte Blanche*
Diane Seuss-Brakeman, *It Blows You Hollow*
Elaine Sexton, *Sleuth; Causeway*
Marc Sheehan, *Greatest Hits*
Heidi Lynn Staples, *Guess Can Gallop*
Phillip Sterling, *Mutual Shores*
Angela Sorby, *Distance Learning*
Matthew Thorburn, *Subject to Change*